MAJESTY

VISIONS FROM THE HEART
OF ELK COUNTRY

ROCKY MOUNTAIN
ELK FOUNDATION

FALCON™

Helena, Montana

CONRAD ROWE

$\mathcal{I}$NTRODUCTION

We will never fully know what the bugle of a bull elk does to another bull hearing it. Or if, on hearing his own bugle echoed off an aspen wall, a bull might feel a certain satisfaction. I suppose some scientist might someday wire up an elk and chart the answer to such questions, but I don't feel I really need to know.

I do sometimes wonder what the human ear finds so meaningful in bugles. Just what keeps us up late some September nights listening for sounds the bull elk sings to the darkness? Is there some secret room in the inner ear where the calls of elk and loons and wolves are processed using a more ancient system? Or maybe those wild vibrations strike the anvil and stirrup of who we really are or were. Maybe bugles are one of the few frequencies that resonate through five hundred years of urbanization, conjuring something like the clear call of the meadowlark, liquid and pure even through the open windows of society speeding by.

There was no good way to package an audio tape with this book. If you have never heard a bugling elk, it is certainly recommended listening. After you have also heard the drumming of elk hooves on a dense forest duff or been surprised in close quarters by a challenge barked, when you have filled your nostrils with the pungence of an elk wallow, then you will turn these pages more slowly, and perhaps hear wild elk between them.

And when you understand these things, you should also know that suburban expansion into critical wildlife winter range is silencing September's bugles in some areas of the West, a trend that will be discomforting in proportion to your enjoyment of this book. The photographs featured here have captured elk at special moments in special places, but elk are just like all the other creatures they share the landscape with—they have many needs, they require habitat to sustain them when snow drifts deep and winds howl cold.

One hundred twenty years ago, few people believed they could kill off a one-ton beast that traveled in herds as long as a five-day horse ride. But bison are mostly symbols and nickels now, and the open spaces they symbolize are more rare than the shaggy beasts themselves.

Elk have learned to fit in the remaining spaces and we don't shoot them from moving steam locomotives, but we're using up their habitat nearly as fast as those railroad labor crews laid track. And like the buffalo shooters leaning out the train windows, we may not see ourselves as actors in this melodrama.

The Rocky Mountain Elk Foundation supports a mission of passing along our rich wildlife heritage to those in the trains behind us by working hard to keep habitat available to wildlife in all the special places where elk live. We believe that nothing could be more important than taking care of what's left of the land around us—places with enough silence yet for those primitive sounds to reach us. We feel that elk best symbolize the wonderful diversity of the western landscape, even if we only hear them on dark September nights. So we publish this book as a celebration of elk, and where they live.

LANCE SCHELVAN
Executive Editor, *BUGLE* magazine
Journal of the Rocky Mountain
Elk Foundation

HUGH H. HOGLE

MEL CUNDIFF

"Many's the time that I've thanked my lucky stars that I live in the heart of elk country."

Don Laubach and Mark Henckel

HENRY H. HOLDSWORTH

*"To those who have always known elk . . .
they will always be symbolic of the high country
of western North America. They are big, handsome
animals, classically proportioned, proud,
intelligent, and very enterprising. . . ."*

ANDY RUSSELL

MICHAEL S. SAMPLE

GARY R. ZAHM

TOM & PAT LEESON

TOM & PAT LEESON

ALAN & SANDY CAREY

DAVID N. OLSEN

"*A small breeze stirs overhead and the quakies sing
a dry, rattling song—like a stepped-on buzzworm,
or a Navajo gourd rattle—just the thing to camouflage
the tom-tom beating of my heart.*

*This is the moment I wait all year, every year, to
re-experience—just me alone, among the elk and aspens.*"

David Petersen

TOM & PAT LEESON

MICHAEL H. FRANCIS

KEN L. JENKINS

"*Maybe I ain't much of a warden, but I sure try. And what I try for is this: that fifty or a hundred years from now, some shiny-eyed kid can run up to some man and say: 'Mister, what did you see in the high country this time out? Are the big elk still there?' And the man can grin and say: 'They sure are, son—there and waitin' for you!*"

JOHN MADSON

TOM & PAT LEESON

DEBI OTTINGER

RON SANFORD

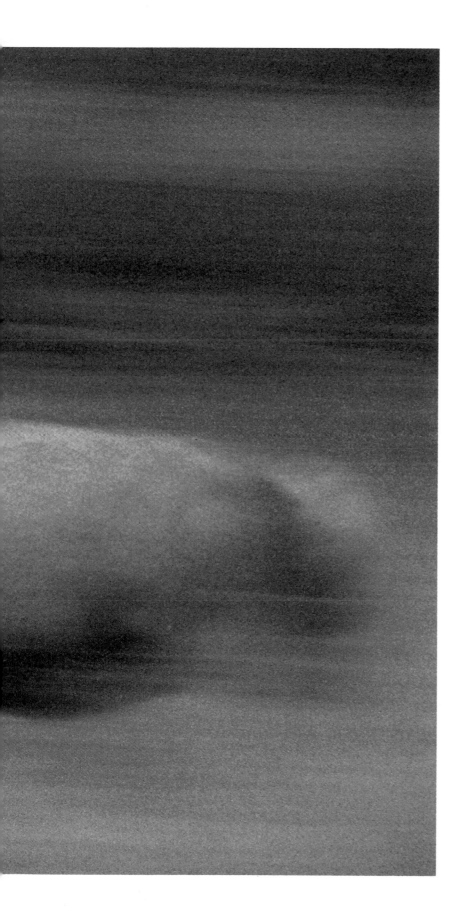

"*With the sudden violence of a big wind combing the tops out of ponderosas, timber cracks and shatters 40 yards in front of you. Hooves drum the earth, hiccupping a sharp cadence of panic. Through the dense aspen you catch a churning blur of black legs, then he moons you— the flash of his rump patch a burnt sienna straight out of the Crayola box. Then there's only noise again, a runaway engine highballing downslope.*"

DAN CROCKETT

"*He was smoking hot and looking for trouble. Neck stretched out and still bugling, his heavy 6-point rack was rotating from side to side as he searched the timber for his foe.*"

ED WOLFF

KEN L. JENKINS

MICHAEL S. SAMPLE

DONALD M. JONES

Henry H. Holdsworth

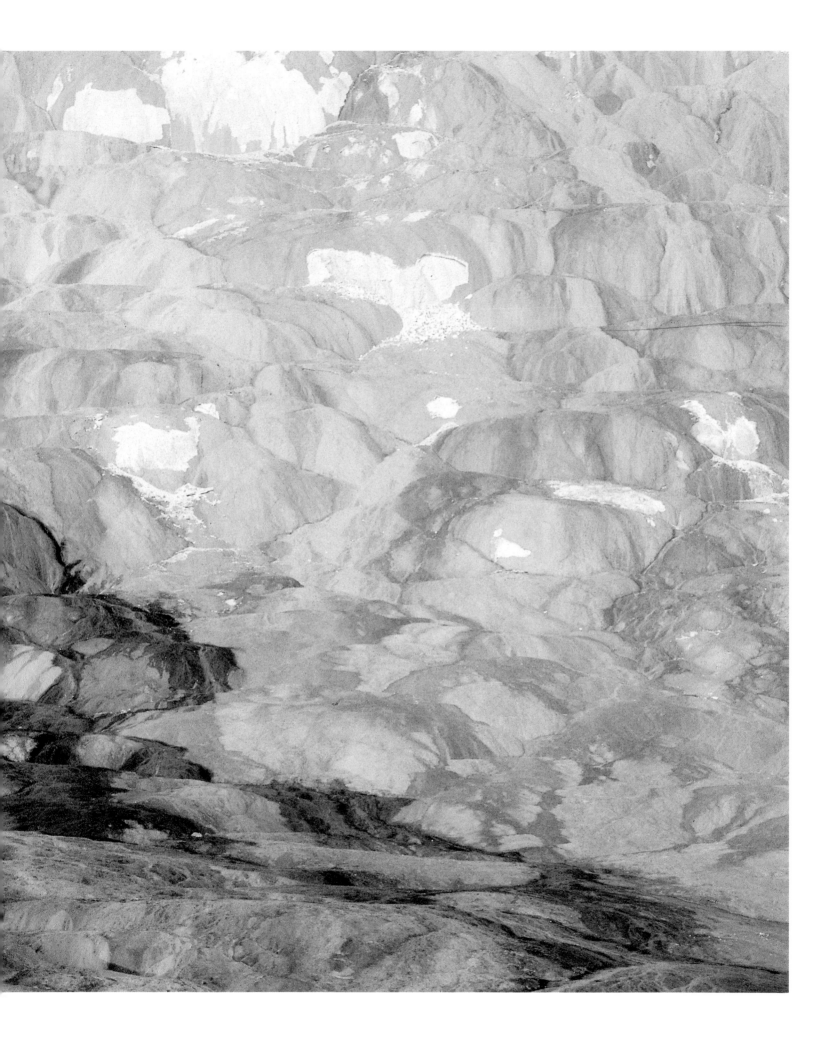

"*In the spring, when they decided to go back, I could see them on the skyline, one right after another, just a constant line of elk across the skyline going back to Yellowstone.*"

BESS ERSKINE

HUGH H. HOGLE

ART WOLFE

MICHAEL S. SAMPLE

"The cow elk is the one who teaches an elk how to be an elk."

SCOTT MCCORQUODALE

D. ROBERT FRANZ

JOHN GERLACH

TOM MURPHY

DONALD M. JONES

40

*"The huge, shapely body . . . was set on legs
that were as strong as steel rods, and yet slender,
clean, and smooth. They were a beautiful dark
brown color, contrasting well with the yellowish
of the body. The neck and throat were garnished with
a mane of long hair and the symmetry of the great
horns set off the fine, delicate lines of the noble head."*

THEODORE ROOSEVELT

TOM & PAT LEESON

HENRY H. HOLDSWORTH

44

"At sunset . . . the moon came up full behind a herd. The setting sun had tinted the mountains pink. The snow was rose, the elk dark against it.

I took pictures until, again, I ran out of film. I know they won't do justice to what I saw."

JIM CARRIER

DENVER A. BRYAN

DENVER A. BRYAN

DEREK HANSON

DONALD M. JONES

"There is no other animal quite as magnificent as an elk. For that I am happy and I'm exquisitely happy that they're here to stay."

JIM ZUMBO

JEFF VANUGA

"An elk can move like a fading shadow in thick timber but when elk forego caution they can crash and clatter like a cavalry charge. . . ."

CHARLES F. WATERMAN

MICHAEL H. FRANCIS

ALAN & SANDY CAREY

"Elk, perhaps more than any
other big game, truly symbolize
wilderness values, and it's the
wilderness expedition that
most hunters dream about. . ."

DWIGHT SCHUH

SHERM SPOELSTRA

ALAN & SANDY CAREY

LINDEN PIEST

LINDEN PIEST

PETE & ALICE BENGEYFIELD

Brian Hay

RON SANFORD

DONALD M. JONES

JEFF VANUGA

" . . . advancing cautiously, we presently through a bush distinguished in the gloom the dark body and antlered head of a real monarch of the forest as he stalked out into an open glade and stared with astonishment at our fire. He looked perfectly magnificent. He was a splendid beast, and his huge bulk, looming large in the uncertain twilight, appeared gigantic."

THE EARL OF DUNRAVEN

TOM & PAT LEESON

FRANK OBERLE

GARY R. ZAHM

DAVID N. OLSEN

MICHAEL JAVORKA

"*In my opinion there is one sound
that typifies wildness, a sound that stirs
contemporary man's primitive instincts
and makes an outdoor experience rich.
It is the deep, gutteral roar of a herd
bull elk rising from the dark of a
north-facing lodgepole jungle.*"

ED WOLFF

"Of all of the various kinds of elk hunting . . .
the most appealing is the hunt during the rut
in late September and early October. It is not only
the marvelous melody that is the bugle of a bull elk,
but the very fact of being there to hear it. It is to hear
the raucous call of the Clark nutcracker as he swoops
from tree to tree . . . . It is to see the sparkle of a million
diamonds as the sun first touches the frosted grass
in early morning, and to feel the slanting rays
of the sun warm on your back at midday.

[It is] To smell the scents of autumn,
the odor of curing grass, decaying wood, and dying
leaves, and the smell of the sun on pine needles. To be
there when the leaves of the quakies turn to gold,
and the mountain maple takes a touch of crimson. . . .

To know the companionship of a good hunting partner
in the lonely elk camp at the end of the day. And to sit
by a roaring campfire with the sparks whirling,
climbing, drifting off into the darkness that envelops
the great, silent land of the wapiti."

BOB HAGEL

RUSS & CHERI EBY

ERWIN & PEGGY BAUER

TOM & PAT LEESON

MICHAEL S. SAMPLE

Michael H. Francis

JEFF VANUGA

DONALD M. JONES

"It was a splendid sight. The great beasts faced each other with lowered horns, the manes that covered their thick necks and the hair on their shoulders bristling and erect. Then they charged furiously, the crash of the meeting antlers resounding through the valley."

THEODORE ROOSEVELT

DONALD M. JONES

RANDY FLAMENT

CONRAD ROWE

Derek Hanson

TOM & PAT LEESON

"*I discovered a band of Elk about half a mile up the mountain. I took my rifle and went to approach them thro the snow 3 ft deep and when within about 250 paces of them they took the wind of me and ran off leaving me to return to my encampment with the consolation that this was not the first time the wind had blown away my breakfast.*"

OSBORNE RUSSELL

CONRAD ROWE

"The bull stomped. Tilting up his black muzzle—laying his splendid, many-tined rack nearly upon his back—he quivered, curled his lips, and discharged a piercing, quavering bugle that culminated in roaring grunts. . . . He ripped the morning air with a calliope of wildness and claimed as his the world around him, forbidding every bull, calling every cow."

MICHAEL FURTMAN

D. Robert Franz

DAVID N. OLSEN

CONRAD ROWE

DEBI OTTINGER

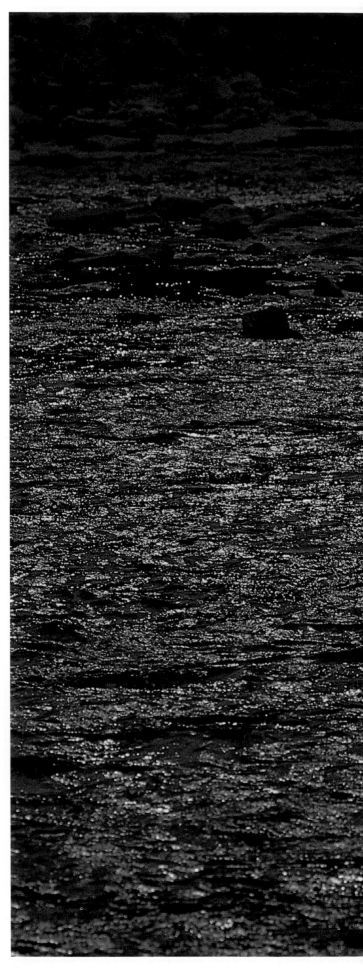

CHASE SWIFT

GARY R. ZAHM

"Terrible tales are told of grown men spending days on end in pursuit of the creature only to find, too late, it was but an apparition of the mind; that the elk, or whatever they mistook to be elk, were only mirages and not flesh and blood animals."

David Darlington

"*The name has never really worked. The Indian name, wapiti, is better, but still not all I would have hoped for. It's as if such short names just can't encompass the grandness here, . . . are too informal to do it justice. A three-letter word doesn't measure up to what this animal displays in glory and grace, unless we call it god. We could do a lot worse than deify something as wild and mystifying as the elk.*"

PAUL SCHULLERY

DAVID N. OLSEN

TOM & PAT LEESON

BILL J. KOPPEN

David N. Olsen

DONNA AITKENHEAD

TIM CHRISTIE

"*I will soon be off again . . .*
The mountains are calling,
and I must go . . ."

JOHN MUIR

David N. Olsen

TIM CHRISTIE

CONRAD ROWE

TOM & PAT LEESON

MICHAEL S. SAMPLE

DAVID N. OLSEN

TIM CHRISTIE

TIM CHRISTIE

111

DONALD M. JONES

TOM MURPHY

DEBI OTTINGER

"*Like the mountain men,
this bull is completely wild and
free. He is nature at its best.
He is life at its best.*"

BOB GERDING

Acknowledgments

THEY MADE IT POSSIBLE

ELK-the name itself evokes visions of hulking beasts bearing tall, broad, symmetrical racks with tines as heavy and sharp as any broadsword. Yet elk are much more than that. They are the embodiment of everything that is wild and free. Few who have heard the bugle of a herd bull challenging all contenders will ever forget it. Fewer still fail to be changed forever by his spirit.

The photographs in this book, highlighted by quotes from the best writers on elk, celebrate this magnificent animal and the beautiful lands they call home.

Majesty: Visions From The Heart Of Elk Country would not have been possible without the skills and efforts of the photographers listed here. Their hard work and diligent pursuit of excellence set their work apart.

To all of the photographers who contributed to *Majesty: Visions From The Heart Of Elk Country,* thank you.

Michael S. Sample, Bill Schneider
Publishers, Falcon Press

Bob Munson
Publisher, Rocky Mountain Elk Foundation

PHOTOGRAPHERS IN MAJESTY: VISIONS FROM THE HEART OF ELK COUNTRY

Erwin, Peggy Bauer
David Blankenship
Denver A. Bryan
Alan, Sandy Carey
Tim Christie
Mel Cundiff
Russ & Cheri Eby
Randy Flament
Michael H. Francis
D. Robert Franz
John Gerlach
Derek Hanson
Brian Hay
Hugh H. Hogle
Henry H. Holdsworth
Michael Javorka
Ken L. Jenkins

Donald M. Jones
Bill J. Koppen
Tom, Pat Leeson
Tom Murphy
David N. Olsen
Debi Ottinger
Linden Piest
Jeffrey Rich
Conrad Rowe
Michael S. Sample
Ron Sanford
Sherm Spoelstra
Chase Swift
Jeff Vanuga
Art Wolfe
Gary R. Zahm

New England Stock Photo

PHOTO CAPTIONS

Page 3
Rocky Mountain elk bull and cows, Montana

Page 5
Rocky Mountain elk bull, Deseret Ranch, Northeast Utah

Page 6, 7
Herd of Rocky Mountain elk, Flat Tops Wilderness, White River National Forest, Colorado

Page 8
Rocky Mountain elk herd, National Bison Range, Montana

Page 9
Rocky Mountain elk cow and calf, Yellowstone National Park, Wyoming

Page 11
Rocky Mountain elk bull, Southern Montana

Page 12
Rocky Mountain elk spike, near Fort Niobrara State Park, Nebraska

Page 13
Rocky Mountain elk bull, Jasper National Park, Alberta, Canada

Page 14
Rocky Mountain elk calf, Yellowstone National Park, Wyoming

Page 15
Rocky Mountain elk calf, Yellowstone National Park, Wyoming

Page 16
Aspen drainage, Monte Cristo Recreation Area, Utah

Page 17
Rocky Mountain elk bull, Jasper National Park, Alberta, Canada

Page 18
Rocky Mountain elk herd, Canadian Rockies, Alberta, Canada

Page 19
Rocky Mountain elk cow, Yellowstone National Park, Wyoming

Page 20, 21
Rocky Mountain elk bull, Jasper National Park, Alberta, Canada

Page 22
Rocky Mountain elk bulls, Western Alberta, Canada

Page 23
Rocky Mountain elk bulls in velvet, Kootenay National Park, British Columbia, Canada

THE PUBLISHERS GRATEFULLY
ACKNOWLEDGE THE FOLLOWING SOURCES

Page 8

from *The Elk Hunter* by Don Laubach and Mark Henckel. Copyright 1989 by Don Laubach and Mark Henckel. Published by Don Laubach.

Page 10

from *The High West* by Andy Russell. Copyright 1974. The Viking Press, New York.

Page 17

from "Among the Elk and the Aspens" by David Petersen in *BUGLE*, Spring 1992.

Page 21

from *Out Home* by John Madson. Copyright 1979. Winchester Press.

Page 25

from "Locomotion" by Dan Crockett in *BUGLE*, Winter 1992.

Page 26, 71

from *Elk Hunting in the Northern Rockies* by Ed Wolff. Copyright 1984 by Ed Wolff.

Page 32

from "Preserving a Legacy" *BUGLE*, Fall 1990.

Page 36

from "In Praise of Cows" by Scott McCorquodale in *Among the Elk: Wilderness Images* by David Petersen. Copyright 1988 by David Petersen. Northland Publishing. Originally published in *BUGLE*, Summer 1987.

Page 41, 80

from *The Hunting and Exploring Adventures of Theodore Roosevelt* by Donald Day. Copyright 1955. Dial Press, Pittsburgh, Pennsylvania.

Page 45

from *Letters From Yellowstone* by Jim Carrier. Copyright 1987 by The Denver Post Corporation. Roberts Rinehart, Inc. Publishers.

Page 50

from "Good News from Elk Country" by Jim Zumbo in *American Hunter Magazine*, November 1992.

Page 52

from *The Part I Remember* by Charles F. Waterman. Copyright 1974 by Charles F. Waterman. Winchester Press, New York.

Page 57

from "The Elk Hunting Tradition" by Dwight Schuh in *BUGLE*, Fall 1984.

Page 66

from *The Great Divide* by The Earl of Dunraven. Copyright 1967 - reprint of 1876 edition. University of Kansas Press, Lawrence, Kansas.

Page 72

from "Elk" by Bob Hagel in *The American Sportsman Treasury*. Copyright 1971. The Ridge Press, Inc., and American Broadcasting Company Merchandising, Inc.

Page 87

from *Osborne Russell, Journal of a Trapper: 1834 - 1843* edited by Aubrey L. Haines. Copyright 1965. University of Nebraska Press, Lincoln, Nebraska.

Page 88

from *Elk* by Daniel J. Cox. Copyright 1992 by Daniel J. Cox. Chronicle Books, San Francisco, California.

Page 95

from "A Scientific Inquiry Regarding the Elk" by David Darlington in *BUGLE*, Spring 1985.

Page 96

from *Mountain Time* by Paul Schullery. Copyright 1984 by Paul Schullery. Nick Lyons Books, New York.

Page 104

from *BUGLE*, Fall 1985.

Page 115

from "Paying My Respects" by Bob Gerding in *BUGLE*, Fall 1988.

"One of the most beautiful facades in the world."

That's how John Wesley Powell described the soaring wall where the Green River emerges from the Book Cliffs. The first white man to float the length of the Green River and all of the Grand Canyon, Powell had seen ten thousand wonders. Yet the beauty and mystery of the Book Cliffs lingered in his mind. And when Powell first stood stunned before the Book Cliffs a century ago, a thousand generations of elk had already passed on their flame and gone back into this magical land.

Today the Rocky Mountain Elk Foundation is working to ensure that the challenges of bugling bulls will echo off these and countless other walls, throughout elk country for generations to come. Because allowing such country to become just a gaudy backdrop for trendy ranchettes is a blasphemy Powell never could have imagined. And because a beautiful facade isn't quite the same without the scream of a golden eagle or the bugle of a bull elk.